"The Lee's"
(another lover story)

By:
Lashonda R. Lee

©2022 Lashonda Lee. All rights reserved. No portion of this book may be reproduced in any form without prior written permission from the copyright owner of this book.

For permission email: **lashonda.lee16@yahoo.com**

Cover by: kingof_designer @fiverr
Edited by: sadeknows @fiverr
ISBN: 9798836610579

ACKNOWLEDGE

To my God, my King, the lover of my soul, the man that has been with me since before the day I was born, my Lord and Savior, Jesus Christ, I owe you my life. One thing I know for sure, without any shallow of a doubt, is that you LOOOOOVVVVVEEEE ME, and I LOOOOOVVVVVEEEE YOU!!! You mean the whole world to me. My main goal in this life, is to make you proud. Thank you so much for saving my life, thank you for choosing me, thank you for loving my imperfect, crazy self. I love you with all my mind, and all my heart, and all my soul, forever.

To my handsome husband, my bestfriend, my right-hand man, thank you. Thank you for being patient with me and putting up with my crazy self. Thank you for everything that you do for our family. Thank you for all your hard work. Thank you for our handsome son (he is just everything). I truly love you guys so much. I wouldn't want to do this life with anyone else by my side. There is nothing in this world that I wouldn't do for you guys. The joy and happiness that y'all bring me is unmeasurable. Y'all are my world and I love you guys to infinity.

To my family, my mom, my dad, my grandmas and grandpas, my brother, my sisters, my best friend, my nephews, my nieces, my aunties, my uncles and all my cousins (on my mom and dad's side of the family) YOOOOOOOO, I did it bay-be!!! Thanks to you all, I am the woman that I always wanted to be. I know that if I ever needed anyone to have my back, y'all got it. I am so grateful for each and everyone of you all, and like my loving uncle T-Smooth always say "I love ya, and there aint a dern thing you can do about it."

To my Washtenaw, Tallman, Fairfield, and California family. OMG, y'all know how to make life so lit. If ever someone needs to have a good time, they can just come around y'all. I can't thank you all enough for the love, kindness, support, protection, mercy and grace that you all have shown towards me and my family. I appreciate and love you all so much.

To my schoolteachers and friends (from Chalmers and Collins), thank you all for making life easy and fun for me. Being around you all, always kept me hopeful. I will always remember every single one of you. I got to learn so much from just being around you all. Having you all a part of my life means the world to me, and I wouldn't change it for anything. I love you all so much.

To my sports family, my coaches, Mr. Gardener, Coach Pharoah, Coach Jesse and Kanesha, Coach Chris, Coach Clark, Veese, Ms. Clora, April, Venus, Rodney, Swauvette, and my teammates, I truly can't thank you all enough for how you came into me, and my sister's lives and helped changed it for the better. You showed us that there was so much more to life than where we came from. You all took great care of us. Y'all invested in us, y'all spent time with us, you all loved us and gave us wisdom that will be with us forever, but most importantly, you believed in us, and you all did this while taking care of your own families. How remarkable is that? I will always honor you all. I love you all so much with all my heart.

To Daddy's Girls International, Ms. Cassandra (my god mom, whom I adore), Ms. Angela, Ms. Arletha, Ms. Debra, Mama Joyce, Sylvia, Ms. Lorri, Ms. Dacia, and Ms. Diane, the words that I have for you all aren't even enough to say thank you for how you came into my life and poured not only your prayers, and your wisdom, but also your genuine love out on me. I can't even count how many times you all showed up for me, over and over again, whenever I needed you all. Not once did you hesitate to do so. Being able to be in your presence is a privilege and I never took one moment for granted. I love you all so much, forever and always.

To my Sinai family, I am so happy that I got to meet you all. There was not one day when I came to work, and it was dull. If I got to see or talk to one of you, my day went amazing. Every one of you always had a way to help uplift me whenever I had a bad day. You taught me how to improve my attitude, think outside the box, get out of my comfort zone, and how to just enjoy life and not take everything so seriously. I can't thank you all enough just for being there. You all are so special to me. I love you all so much.

To my pastors and their wives, my church family (New Life) and all the beautiful women that I got to connect with more outside the four walls of the church, Princess, Sharell, Makayla, Chari, Ms. Shirley, Michelle, Necia, Ashley, Keisha, Lonnie, Rainbow, Tameika, Key-Key, Shay, Brandy, Jasmine, Jessica, Cherita, Destiny, and Jayda, I truly love you all so much. The fact that you all accepted me just as I am, warms my heart. Not once did I have to pretend to be anyone else around you all. Y'all are such a breath of fresh air. The wisdom, and the resources and knowledge you all poured into me, made me wiser, valuable, and richer. I couldn't have prayed for a better church family. Thank you so much for everything that you have done for me. I got nothing but so much love for you all.

To my in-laws (there are so many of you all), my mom, my pops, my sisters, my niece and my nephew, my grandparents, my aunties, my uncles, and all one million of my cousins (literally), WOW! YOU ALL ARE AMAZINGGGGGG. I couldn't have prayed for better in-laws. You all accepted me with open arms. The love and support you have given me, my husband and our son, is (MY GOD) out of this world. Please don't stop being who you are. Y'all take that word FAMILY very seriously, which has taught me how to love and appreciate my own family even more. I love you all so much, and in the words of my beloved uncle, "It ain't a darn thing you can do about it."

To my home girls Terrinicka, Ebony, Melissa, Chardae, Thati, and Thati, oh my gosh, y'all are my girls forever. I only have to mention once that I need to get something done; you girls are on it. I can share my dreams and goals with you all. If I ever need encouragement, I can come to you all. If I ever need to just have a great time, I can come to you all. I know you all have my best interest at heart. Your love for me is so genuine, and I won't ever let that go. I love you all so much.

To my readers and supporters, I know we don't know each other yet, but I hope that through my book, you all will get to know me a little more. I am so grateful for each and every one of you. I can't thank you all enough for your love and support. I hope you enjoy reading my story. I got nothing but love for you all to.

"It takes a village to raise a child."
This is my village, and they definitely helped raise me.

Table of Contents:

"The Beginning" 3

"The Job" 8

"Another Job" 14

"The Crew" 20

"Favor" 26

"Finding My Way" 30

"New Life" 35

"A Test of Faith" 40

"Shifting My Focus" 44

"In Denial" 50

"A Decision to Make" 54

"A Decision" 59

"Another Beginning" 63

"The End" 67

"I tried to put my foot in this book y'all. Hope you like it."

Love Always
-Shonda

"There is hope, even when your brain tells you there isn't."

-John Green

"The Beginning"
Chapter 1:

So, there I was, sitting on my aunt's porch after a long walk from my mom's house. I had just come outside so I could finish job hunting. It was about 12:00pm, on a very hot sunny day in the middle of July. I sat on that porch feeling so defeated. I had been searching for a job for the last five months and I was getting nowhere. My thoughts started kicking my butt. *"So, you really haven't found a job yet? It can't be that hard sis. So many people your age been had jobs. Girl, you might as well just give it up."* After that last thought to myself, I simply bowed my head and gave up. As soon as my eyes started to water, I felt the presence of a white truck pulling up and then stopping directly in front of me.

A familiar voice called out and said, "B-Bubs, what are you doing out here this early?"

I blinked really quickly to draw back the tears that were about to fall before I lifted my head, put a huge smile on my face, then got up off the porch and ran to the truck.

"Hey Coach Pharoah," I said. "I'm just out here getting ready to finish job hunting."

He looked at me, smiled and said, "Well don't give up, you will find something. Here…" he reached into his pockets and pulled out a $20 bill and gave it to me.

I smiled super hard and said, "Thank you so much."

I walked off feeling too happy and confused, trying to figure out what just happened and who was listening to me. As I was getting ready to sit back down on my aunt's porch, I heard another familiar voice call out from behind me saying, "Shonda, what are you doing out here this early?" It was my cousin April, whom I am always so excited to see.

"Oh, hey cousin," I turned around and said, "I'm about to finish job hunting."

Once I said that, she walked on the porch to where I was, grabbed my hand and didn't say a word. We power walked all the way down Fairfield to make our way toward Mt. Sinai Hospital. She didn't let my hand go and I didn't let hers go either. When we finally made it to the Sinai Community Institute building (also known as SCI), we approached the security guard sitting at the front desk.

"Hi, how can I help you all," the security guard asked as we walked toward her.

"Hey, is Montanez in?" my cousin asked.

"You mean Montez?" the security guard responded.

"Yes," my cousin said.

"Well, he isn't here today, but I can get someone else to help you all. Just wait here for a moment please," she responded as she got up and walked away.

My cousin and I stood there staring into space waiting for her to return. I never asked my cousin any questions and she never gave me any answers. I was just trusting the fact that she was leading me in the right direction.

"Hi, are you all here for the youth program?" a man came out and asked us.

"She is," my cousin said as she gave me a little shove to stop being scared and follow the man.

"Meet me back on Fairfield when you are finished," she added.

"Okay," I responded with a look on my face that said, *"so you just gone leave me up here with this man?"* Instead of responding she turned and walked away.

"You can follow me young lady," he said as he held the door open.

"Okay," I responded. "Now here is a package for you to fill out." He handed me a folder full of papers. "You will print your name here, sign and date it here, personal info here, sign and date here. I need your birth certificate, state I.D. and social security card."

"Oh, I don't have my birth certificate or social security card with me," I said as I cut him off. He was speaking so fast.

"Okay, that's fine. Just bring it back with you on Monday when you start orientation."

"Orientation! Oh my gosh!" I thought to myself. *"I have a job. I have a job. I cannot believe this."* At this point, I was filling out my paperwork and I was super excited and filled with so much joy. I made my way back to Fairfield to look for my cousin to tell her the good news and she saw me first.

"So, when do you start?" she called out.

I looked at her and smiled so hard and asked, "How did you know I would get the job?"

"Because I was trying to sign up for it myself, but they told me I was too old."

She then went on to let me know that they were trying to hire at least four hundred youth from a large grant they received for that summer. I didn't know how she knew so much, nor did I ask. I just took her word for it, and I started spreading the word. I knew that if I was having trouble looking for a job, others were to, and I was more than delighted to tell them where to go for a great opportunity. I went home feeling super accomplished. I couldn't believe what just happened to me.

"I GOT A JOB!"

"I'm so glad trouble don't last always. He may not come when you want him, but he's always on time."

Song by:
-Rev. Timothy Wright
"Trouble don't last always"

"The Job"

Chapter 2:

It was now Monday, and I needed to hurry up and get up so I could walk to work and be on time. It took me about forty minutes to get there by foot, but I didn't mind because I was used to walking everywhere. I was really scared because I didn't know what to expect. I started doubting myself again. When I finally made it to SCI for orientation, I opened the door to where it was being held and I saw a large group of youth and familiar faces waiting for the orientation to get started. Seeing them made the fear and nervousness disappear as I made my way to my seat. I didn't feel alone anymore. Just seeing so many other youth was a relief. I was able to see for the first time, that opportunities did exist for people like me, you just needed to be in the right place at the right time.

Orientation was beginning and the guy that gave me my application package was hosting it. I just knew that I would have plenty of questions because he talked so fast like he was in a rush. He started speaking and you can bet your last dollar I was right. I didn't understand a word he was saying, nor was I trying to. I just told myself that I could wait until orientation was over to ask the young lady that I needed to give my birth certificate and social security card to about what to do.

I approached her and said, "Excuse me, I just have a quick question. Are we supposed to report straight to our job site or come here first then go there?"

"Oh no love, you will report straight to your job site Mon-Fri from 9-5, but on your lunch break on Fridays, you will stop up here and get your 7-day bus pass for the following week." "Oh wow, we are getting 7-day bus passes to get back and forth to work?" I asked with a big smile on my face.

"Yes," she said as we both laughed.

"Thank you," I replied as I handed her my documents.

"You're welcome," she responded as she got up to walk away and make copies. I was so happy about the news. Before this conversation, I thought I would be walking back and forth to work every day until I got paid because I didn't have money for bus fare, and I was not about to ask anyone for help. Now that I had my every need being met, I had no room for excuses.

When the next day came, I went to report to my job site. Upon arrival, I saw some of my friends and other youth from the orientation. We had to report to the SOLIS building on Homan and Arthington, which wasn't too far from my mom's house.

"Goodmorning you all, my name is Ms. Sanders, and I am your supervisor for this job site. We will meet here every morning, Mon-Fri from 9-5. All I need you all to do is walk around the neighborhood and pass out these flyers. You can all go together or split up into groups. You can meet back here at twelve, sign your time sheets and then go home. Don't worry, you will still get your full-time hours."

"Wait, what? This sounds too good to be true. That's all we have to do every day? My god, if this isn't the easiest job

ever," I thought to myself. I didn't miss a day of work. I made sure of it. I was meeting new people left and right and I was super excited about it. A few weeks later, our job site supervisor chose me to work with her for her magazine company because she was impressed with how dedicated I was to the small assignment she gave us. I had never done anything like this before and I couldn't wait to see what it entailed.

Unfortunately, the summer was coming to an end and I was not looking forward to it. I wished it could have lasted a little longer. I started getting worried again because I didn't know what I was going to do next. I didn't want to go back to doing nothing or being nothing. With this concern still on my mind, I overheard some of my co-workers talking about a job readiness class one day. Apparently, SCI was offering this to the youth for free for anyone that wanted to join.

"I don't think I'm going to do it because we are not getting paid for it," one of the guys said.

"I want to do it, where can I sign up?" I chimed in.

"At SCI," one of my co-workers responded.

As soon as I got off work that day, I walked right up to SCI to figure out how to sign up for that program. I didn't have time to wait on the bus, I was faster, and I needed to get on that roster before there was no more space left. I quickly made it to SCI and a knock on the right door was about to change my life forever.

[Knock, knock, knock]

"Hey there, how can I help you," a tall, beautiful, black woman said as she opened the door.

"Hello, I was coming to sign up for the job-readiness program that's about to start soon," I responded smiling.

"Oh, ok. Come on in and go sit at the round table over in the corner to your left and I will bring a package over for you to sign."

She walked over to her desk as I started making my way over to the round table. Not once had it crossed my mind that at this round table, I would be present for countless future meetings, lunch gatherings and birthday celebrations.

"Alright, here you go. I am going to go through this with you because it is a lot to fill out and sign," she said. She took a seat beside me and started helping me with the application. "Okay, I need you to print your first and last name here. Fill this information out here. Sign here and date here. Now this class will be held here at SCI in town hall A every Saturday from 9-2. You will get meal tickets for lunch and a bus card to get to and from class every week," she said as she gave me the ins and outs about the program. Once she finished, she asked, "Now do you have any questions for me?"

"No," I responded with a huge smile on my face.

"Okay, well I will see you Friday when you come and pick up your check," she said as she got up to walk back to her desk. As I was leaving, I noticed that I didn't know her name. I decided to stop at the security desk and ask.

"Excuse me, do you know the woman's name that runs the youth program?"

"Yes, it's Ms. Cassandra," the security guard responded.

"Okay, thanks so much," I said as I walked away. From that day forward, I made sure I never forgot it. My life was changing rather quickly, and I was super excited about it, plus, there was even more waiting for me.

"Hard work always pays off, whatever you do."

–Dustin Lynch

"Another Job"
Chapter 3:

"Okay everyone, class was great today. Don't forget that next Saturday we will have two guest speakers and we are also doing mock interviews. Please make sure you all practice because we are not taking these interviews lightly. We will see you all next week," one of our instructors said as class ended.

I was not good with interviews. I always found myself stumbling over my words and losing my train of thoughts when asked a question. During that whole week, I decided to google and watch YouTube videos on how to perfect an interview. I would practice in the mirror as much as possible with the interview worksheet my instructors gave us.

"Well Lashonda, tell me about yourself?" I asked staring in the mirror.

"Well, I am nineteen years old.... ugh nooooooo," I said, "don't start with *well*. Let's try it again," I instructed myself. "I am nineteen years old, I, ummm, graduated from high school. Noooooooo, don't say *um*," I corrected. I sighed feeling slightly frustrated. "You know what, I'll just finish this tomorrow."

"Are you okay Shonda?" my baby sister Erica asked as she walked past the bathroom.

We both started laughing and I said, "nope girl, I'm trying to get these questions right for this practice interview I got coming up in class this Saturday."

"Here, let me see your paper. I'll ask you the questions and you can just answer them like you are in a real interview. Maybe that will help you."

"Oh my gosh, thank you so much ma-ma. I sure can use your help." For two good hours, we went back and forth asking and answering questions. My baby sister helped me out every day right up until it was Saturday. When the day came, I was confident. I practiced as much as I could, and I was ready for whatever.

"Goodmorning everyone. Today, our two guest speakers are here to speak with you all about this program and how it has helped change their lives. Let's give them our undivided attention please," one of the instructors announced as class began.

"Goodmorning, my name is Vernon, and I am Harold." Then Vernon spoke… "We both went through this class to help get us to where we are today." As he continued speaking, I couldn't help but notice that I had seen these two guys before. I know I saw them, but I couldn't figure out where. However, I didn't dwell on it since I couldn't allow it to throw me off. I had to nail this interview today because I didn't want to feel like a failure. I practiced for this all week.

"Alright, let's give them a big round of applause and thank them so much for coming out and speaking with us," one of the instructors said after he stood up to clap. "Now, for the most important part of the day, mock Interviews. Starting with the first table in the back of the room, start counting," the instructor said as he pointed at the table in the back that I was sitting at.

"One," the first girl said.

"Two," the next girl said.

"Three," I said thinking to myself, *"now why would he choose this table to go first when I sat back here to go last."* The counting continued until everyone in the room had a number.

"Okay, let's go number one," the instructor called out. The first girl went and I thought she nailed it.

"You did good, but you could have done better. You were pausing for long periods of time and you weren't making enough eye contact. Let's continue to work on that, great job though. Next."

"Are you serious?" I thought to myself. I just crossed my fingers. I just felt like I needed to do great. The second girl went, and I got increasingly nervous because it was almost my turn. I decided to take the feedback he was giving them, and I applied it to myself.

"Good job, but let's work on not saying 'um' too much," he told the second girl.

"Next."

I shook my fear off and decided to pretend that he was my baby sister helping me. As I made my way up to the front, I told myself, *"You got this girl."* My instructor greeted me and shook my hand as I sat down. He started asking me questions as I replied with the appropriate answers. He gave me eye contact; I gave it right back. We were up there flowing. I felt so relieved when it was over as I sat there nervously waiting to hear his feedback.

"Wow, now that's how you do an interview. Y'all give her a hand," he said.

I smiled super hard and got up and walked back to my seat feeling like I just won a medal. Our instructor finished doing the interviews. Once everyone had a chance to go, he stood up and said, "the purpose of us doing these mock interviews was to see who has been paying attention and taking this class seriously. Numbers three and ten, please step in the hallway for a quick second."

I wasn't sure why we had to go in the hallway, but I got my fingers crossed, hoping it was good. Me and number ten made our way to the hallway as the instructor came out behind us and closed the door.

"The reason I called you two out here is because you both did a great job during your interviews, and I can tell that you both went home and practiced and took it seriously. With that being said, I want to offer you both a position to work here in the SCI building."

"What?" I said really loud.

"Shhh, shhh, shhhhhhhh," the instructor whispered. "I know it's exciting, so what do you all say?"

"Yes," we both responded.

"Alright. Congratulations to both of you. I need you to stay ten minutes later after class today to fill out some paperwork. You will start on Monday. Not this Monday coming up, but the following Monday, and you will ask for Ms. Cassandra. She will be expecting you."

"Ms. Cassandra? I know her," I thought to myself. "Thank you so much," I said with a gigantic smile on my face. After the discussion, we returned to the class to finish up. Once I finished signing my paperwork for my new job, I went home to get some rest because I was overwhelmed with the great news I had just received. I couldn't wrap my mind around it. I guess that saying is true. Hard work does pay off.

"First impressions are not always accurate."

-Unknown

"The Crew"
Chapter 4:

[Knock, knock, knock] [door opens]
"Goodmorning Ms. Cassandra, I am here for one of the youth positions," I said super loud with a big smile on my face laughing.

"Goodmorning child. Come on in here so I can show you where you will be sitting," she responded smiling back at me. "And congratulations," she added as we started walking towards my new office. "You and Bryant will share a desk. You will meet him sometime today. You can hang your coat up over there on anyone of those coat racks. Have a seat right here and I will be right back with your login for this computer."

"Goodmorning," I heard a familiar voice say as he entered the same cubicle I was in.

"Goodmorning," Ms. Cassandra and I responded at the same time.

I had noticed that it was the guy who hosted my orientation. A few seconds later, I felt him stand behind me and tap me super hard on my right shoulder.

[Tap, tap, tap]

"Excuse me, is this your coat?" he asked with my coat hanging in his hand.

"Yes, and why are you tapping me that hard?" I asked with an attitude as I swung my chair around to look at him.

"Okay, well you see this coat rack right here, this is mine. You can put your coat on anyone of these other ones," he responded with an attitude as he hung my coat on a different coat rack. I turned around, rolled my eyes, and stared into my computer.

"Look, we just came here to get a"

"Who told you, you could sit at my desk," an unfamiliar voice yelled at me interrupting the conversation that I was having with myself.

"Ms. Cassandra said I could sit here," I responded with another attitude. "Aw nawl, see she going to have to do something about this because this is not about to happen," he said as he walked away.

I quickly got up, grabbed my coat and put it on. I didn't have time for this. It was too early in the morning for this kind of drama.

"Lashonda," Ms. Cassandra called out to me.

"Yes," I responded as I hurried to unzip my coat and take it back off because I didn't want her to know that I was about to leave.

"Can you come here for a minute please?"

"Coming," I said.

Once I made it to her office, I saw the same guy that just yelled at me for sitting at his desk standing beside her.

"Bryant has something that he wants to say to you."

"Really Ms. Cassandra?" he said laughing.

"Say it," she told him.

"I'm sorry for yelling at you. You can sit at that desk. I barely be at that desk anyways."

[Bryant] Hold on now, I don't remember it happening like that.

[Me] Boy, yes it did, now get out my book, I'm telling the story.

Now where was I, oh yeah, so he apologized, and I stared at him with a fake smile and said, "it's ok."

"Can I go now Ms. Cassandra? Please," he asked.

"Boy, go and get out of my office," she said. "You don't have to worry about him, he doesn't mean no harm." She then got up to show me what I would be doing for the rest of the day. Lunchtime rolled around rather quickly, and I didn't bring any food to eat, nor did I have money to get any, so I decided to go and sit in the resource center (also known as the computer lab) to spend my lunch break in there until it was time for me to go back to work.

"Ha, ha, ha, ha, bro you stupid," one voice said to another.

I entered the resource room and to my surprise, it was the two guys from my Saturday class. I just smiled and pulled out my chair to sit down as one of them said, "Girl, what you doing? You can't sit in here."

I looked at him and said, "Boy, don't you play with me."

"Aw nawl bro, don't play with her, she got an attitude problem," Bryant said as they all started laughing, walking out of the resource room. I started cracking up laughing too because in that moment, I realized that Ms. Cassandra was right. Bryant didn't mean any harm and I had nothing to worry about. They closed the door behind them, and I turned the computer on to get on Facebook.

A few minutes later, I heard the door open. "Hey Lashonda, what are you doing down here by yourself?" When I turned around to look, I saw that it was Montez (the man everyone was crazy about). I remember seeing him when he was talking to Ms. Cassandra at her desk.

"Oh, I just wanted to use the computer," I said lying straight through my teeth. Child, I was hungry, but I was too embarrassed to say it, especially since I had just met them.

"Aw nawl, come down here and eat with us. We got plenty of food. You don't have to be by yourself. Whatever it is that you need, you can ask any one of us," he said.

"Okay, thanks," I responded with a smile.

"Come on, let's go so you can meet the rest of the team as well," he said as he held the door open. As I got up to follow him to the town hall, I noticed why Montez was everyone's favorite. He has a heart of gold, and it quickly made him my favorite too. We entered the town hall and he introduced me to the rest of the team. "That's Vernon, Harold, Bryant, Ms. Amanda, and Ms. Cassandra," he said as he pointed everyone out. I felt like I fitted right in. My day was turning out to end way better than what it had started. I learned that day, that first impressions aren't always accurate. Some people just need some time for you to get to know them better, whilst others are not as kind as they present themselves to be when you first meet them.

"I don't want to be anything other than what I been trying to be lately. All I have to do is think of me, and I'll have peace of mind."

Song by:
-Gavin DeGraw
"I don't want to be"

"Favor"
Chapter 5:

Although the guys and I always got caught having a great time at work, we made sure we got our jobs done first. So many people felt as though we should have been fired because we joked and played a lot, but we were just being ourselves. They couldn't wrap their minds around why our supervisors loved us so much. One day, Ms. Cassandra called a team meeting in the resource room and said that the President and CEO (Alan Channing) of the hospital wanted to meet with us for lunch.

"Don't y'all go in this meeting with all that playing and joking around," she said. "I need y'all to take this seriously because anything could happen." After she said that, you could literally hear a pen drop. Maybe we all thought the same thing. *"This was it. They done went and got the President and CEO to fire us." "Oh, Lord, I don't want to lose this job, I love this job," I thought to myself.* The pressure was on. We were on our best behavior that whole morning. We didn't know what was about to happen. I was hoping noon took its time to come, but nope, it was moving rather quickly. When 12 o'clock came, we were quieter than quiet as we made our way to one of the town halls to meet with Mr. Alan.

"Goodafternoon, my name is Alan Channing," he said as we walked into the town hall to sit across from him at the table. "I wanted to meet with you all because I was really impressed with the bow tie that you wore to the meeting last week," he said as he pointed at Harold. We all laughed as it felt like a huge weight had been lifted off our shoulders. He then went on to say that he would like to meet with us once a month to get to know us better and he did it faithfully. We all were in shock because who were we, that the President and CEO of the hospital wanted to meet with us once a month to get to know us more. Mr. Alan is the true definition of: when someone loves you, they will make time for you. Once our meeting had ended, everyone wanted to know what in the world was going on. Why did the President and CEO of the hospital want to meet with us, the kids that don't do anything, but play all day. We never cared what people thought about us because we knew that if we weren't getting our jobs done, we never would have had one. This workday had come to an end, and I was just ready to go home to get some rest, to wake up the next day and do it all over again.

Once I made it home, on this particular day, I heard laughter and a new voice coming from the kitchen as I opened the front door. I put a huge smile on my face because I wanted my smile to be the first thing this new person saw when they saw me. I walked into the kitchen, sat my bag down, unzipped my coat and then said,

"Heeeyyy, who is this?"

"Heeeyyy, my name is Princess, and this is my son and daughter, and they are your cousins," she responded. I walked over to give them all a hug and she hugged me back and said,

"Oh wow, you are the first person to embrace us this way since we been here."

I smiled at her again and said, "well, it was really nice to meet you all," and then I left to go upstairs to my room. Before she left to go home, she made sure she came to get my name and number.

I went to sleep that night with a lot on my mind. I knew that the time was near for me to make some changes in my personal life and when that time came, I didn't hesitate to make them.

"A closed mouth won't get fed."

-Kevin Daniel

"Finding My Way"
Chapter 6:

Right in the middle of a bad winter, I made a conscious decision to leave the place that I knew as home. I had made up in my mind that I will not continue to live in dysfunction. I packed up everything I had, and it was just me and my little red bag. I decided to call my cousin April and ask if I could come and stay with her until I found my own place, and she was delighted to have me. The only thing was that the place she was staying at, she was house sitting for one of her relatives, and they would be home soon, which meant we all had to leave when they came. She wanted me to come home with her, but she lived too far away, and I didn't want to leave my job. I went to work every day, still smiling and laughing, hoping that I would find an apartment. Soon, the day had come for us to leave. I honestly didn't know what I was going to do and going back was out the question. I started packing my bags and my cousin came into the room to where I was.

"Shonda," she said. "I called Shirley and asked her if you could come and stay with her until you find your own place and she said yes, she is waiting for you."

"Oh my gosh cousin, thank you so much for real because I didn't know what I was going to do," I said to her while I was zipping up my coat.

"I know what you're going through cousin, and you are going to be ok."

By her saying those reassuring words, I really felt like it was going to be ok. Before she dropped me off at my aunt's house, I went to the bathroom and I cried. I cried because I couldn't believe that running from house to house was something I would be doing at the age of 20. I hurried and wiped my eyes dry so no one would know that I was crying. I left out the bathroom and smiled like I always did and said, "let's go," as if I were super excited.

After we made it to my aunt's house, I knocked on the door and she opened it. "Hey baby," she greeted. "Now you know if you ever need me, I will always be here for you. Come on in so I can show you where you will be sleeping."

"Okay, thank you," I said smiling dragging my little red bag behind me. Once I got settled in, I laid down and I cried again because I didn't want to be a burden to anyone. I got up the next morning and I went to work trying to hide behind my smile. Later that day, Ms. Cassandra called me to her office.

"What's wrong? Are you okay?" she asked.

I smiled and said, "yes, why do you say that?"

"Because you don't seem like your bubbly self today, that's all."

I smiled again and reassured her that I was ok. For some reason, Ms. Cassandra didn't believe a word I told her. Instead, she told me to follow her to the town hall. We sat down and she just stared at me. She wasn't the type to just believe anything you told her. She was going to figure it out. She knew exactly when I was lying and telling the truth and that day, she knew I was lying.

"You don't have to lie to me," she said. I know when something is not right with one of y'all." I finally caved in, and I broke down crying again. I told her everything I was going through and she prayed for me like I never heard anyone pray before. That day, she taught me about prayer and a little more about Jesus. We eventually went to the resource center after our talk and she started helping me look for apartments. She asked the guys if they could help as well. Montez offered to let me stay at his place while he was out of town, but it was too far, and I didn't know how to travel that well yet, and Ms. Cynthia C. (I met her while I was working in the WIC playroom), she drove me around as often as she could from place to place, helping me look for apartments. Once I opened up, it was like help started pouring from out of nowhere and I started to truly feel better again. All I needed was for one person to see me and she did. Ms. Cassandra (my god mom) made sure we talked regularly. She dedicated most of her lunch breaks checking up on me and making sure I was ok. She didn't let anything get in the way of her being there for me.

I stayed with my aunt for about two months before I got the call I was waiting for. "Hello, hi Lashonda, I have some great news for you. I was able to talk to the landlord and he finally said yes, you can get the apartment. If you can meet me today, you can sign your lease and get your keys."

"OMG, thank you, thank you so much," I said as my heart dropped. I couldn't believe the landlord finally said yes after giving me a hard time about my age. I gave him my word that he wouldn't have to worry. I told my god mom the good news, and she took me to meet with the agent on our lunch break to get my keys. When I got off work, I went home to my new apartment and stood in the middle of the living room and just smiled. I couldn't believe this was happening for me. I laid on the floor that night staring up at the ceiling, wondering what was next. I just couldn't seem to sit still. I felt like I always needed to accomplish something. I prayed that night, asking God to find me a church home. Little did I know, that prayer was already answered, and a phone call from the right person was about to lead me straight to him.

"I never knew, I could be so happy. I never knew, I'd be so secure. Because of your love, life has brand new meaning. It's gonna be a brighter day, brighter day!"

Song by:
-Kirk Franklin
"Brighter Day"

"New Life"

Chapter 7:

[They be like smooth, What? Can you teach me how to dougie] [song by Cali Swag District] my ringtone played while my phone was sitting on the counter.

"Hello," I said as I answered the phone.

"Hey Shonda, this me, Princess. What are you doing today?" she asked.

"Oh, heeeeyyyy Princess. I'm actually about to go to this church down the street from my job."

"Ok, I was calling to see if you wanted to go to church with me today, it starts at 1:30?" she asked.

"Okay, sure. The one I go to lets out at 12. I should be home by 12:30," I responded.

"Ok, send me your address and I will be there by one to pick you up."

"Okay, see ya soon."

After we hung up, I started debating on whether I wanted to go to the church down the street from my job, but I ended up going anyways.

I finally made it home from church around 12:20 and I couldn't wait to get out of my church clothes and heels, but then I remembered that I was going to attend church with Princess, so I just sat down on my futon and watched tv until she came.

[They be like smooth]

"Hello," I said as I quickly answered the phone.

"Hey Shonda, I'm downstairs," she responded.

"Okay, here I come."

I hurried and put my heels back on and rushed downstairs.

"You know you don't have to dress like that," Princess called out to me as I was coming out the door.

"Are you serious?" I said louder than I expected.

"Yes, it's literally a come as you are church," she said.

"Okay, wait here and I will be right back."

I ran upstairs so fast. I changed into a tank top, jeans and flip flops. I came back downstairs ready to go, feeling so much like myself. I got in the car, and we made our way to Roosevelt and Halsted, to the church that became my church home forever. I really couldn't wait to see what was to this church since I could really come as I am. As she parked in the parking lot, I started looking around because things started looking too familiar. When we crossed the street, I saw on the side of UIC, the cosmetology school that I dropped out of. I started laughing to myself like *"oh wow."* We walked into the UIC building, making our way toward the auditorium where service was being held and oh my gosh y'all, it was super lit. I had never seen so many people in my life. *"What is this, a club for Jesus?"* I thought to myself. We walked into the auditorium, and I couldn't believe my eyes. The main lights were out, but the lights on the stage were lit up in all the right places. The praise team was jamming/singing, "Gooood great God, forever. There's nobody like him, forever you're my God." My shoulders started moving up and down and side to side as we were making our way to our seats. The dance team was snapping. It was everything.

"Hallelujah, hallelujah. Can you hug at least three to five people around you and tell them it's a blessing to be in the house of God," the pastor said as he came on stage. As he continued talking, I realized that I knew his voice.

"OMG, that's Pastor Hannah from 1390 with Angela Martin. My mom listened to them every morning before we went to school," I said excitedly to Princess as we sat down. "I did not know he had a church." I was all ears at this point. He bought the word of God forth and it was so amazing. It blew me away that I was actually able to understand what he was saying. I was crying and everything. I told myself that this was it; this was the church for me.

"Do you want to stand in line and give him a hug?" Princess asked as service had ended.

"What, girl we can hug this man?" I responded with so much excitement.

"Yes," she replied laughing.

We stood in line waiting for our turn to hug Pastor Hannah and I was just in awe.

"Hey Pastor," Princess said as she gave him a hug. She then turned to me and said, "this is Shonda, and this is her first time here."

He smiled, gave me a hug, and said, "make sure you come back now."

I smiled back and said, "I will."

We left shortly after so Princess could take me home. She went out of her way every Sunday to make sure she bought me to church with her. She also introduced me into so many other amazing women, who also went out of their way on Sundays or days I signed up to serve, to bring me to church with them. Princess, Sharrell, Makayla, Ashley, Chari, Key-Key, Shay, Kiesha, Michelle, Tameika, & Lonnie, those are my girls.

I couldn't wait to get to work the next day so I could tell the guys about this amazing church I went to. I started thinking about how everything was happening in my life and pinpointed it back to Jesus. I didn't know much about how he operated, but I sure was about to find out more.

"Have I not commanded you? Be strong and courageous. Do not be afraid; do not be discouraged, for the Lord your God will be with you wherever you go."

(NIV) Joshua 1:9

"A Test of Faith"
Chapter 8:

Monday was here and I was super excited to make my way to work to tell the guys about where I went Sunday. After a good twenty-minute walk, I finally made it to work. I opened the door to where my desk was and said real loud, "Goodmorning knuckleheads."

"Lashonda, why are you so loud?" Vernon, my twin godbrother responded as he started cracking up (we got the same birthdays y'all and he always had my back, that's why I call him my twin godbrother).

"What's going on?" I asked as I pulled out my chair to sit down.

"Ms. Cassandra said she got to talk to us about the budget. She wants us to meet her in the resource center in ten minutes," Vernon responded.

"Where is Bryant?" I asked.

"He's coming," he said.

Two minutes later, Bryant walked through the door, and we updated him on the meeting with Ms. Cassandra in the resource room. Silence gripped the air as we all started making our way down the hallway.

"Goodmorning everyone. Take a seat," Ms. Cassandra greeted us on our way in. "I called this meeting because I need to talk to you all about the budget cut. What that means is that the government has cut the funding for the program that you all are getting paid under, so we must make some changes."

"Ok, cool, we're not getting fired," I said to myself as she continued speaking. "Instead of having you all take pay cuts, we decided to just change your work schedule. Everyone will come in four days a week instead of five. Bryant and Lashonda, you will come in Mon-Thurs, 9-5. Vernon and Harold, you will have Tues-Fri 9-5. That way, every day is covered during the week and someone will always be here. Any questions?"

"No." We all shook our heads.

"Okay, so you all can go back to work. This new schedule won't take place until next week," she said right before she ended the meeting.

"Well, that went better than I thought it would," I said out loud to the guys as we were walking back to our desks. They just looked at me, shook their heads and smiled. Once we returned to our desks, they started sharing why they were feeling so down. I never thought about the budget cut how they thought about it. *"Having a little income was better than having no income,"* I said to myself. "Sooooowah, I guess this isn't a good time for me to tell y'all that I went to a raw church yesterday?" I asked interrupting them."

"Nooooo Lashonda," Vernon said cracking up as he walked away. The rest of us started laughing too. I always had a funny way of lightening the mood. I went home that day, sulking in my feelings after thinking about what the guys were saying. *"You can't tell me that I'm about to get put out after I just came from church,*" I said to myself as I was entering the house. "*What if they decide to let us go? What am I going to do Jesus?*" I thought my life was about to fall apart again, but this situation was out of my control, so I decided to let go and let God have his way because He always knew what to do.

"You can't start the next chapter of your life if you keep re-reading the last one."

-Unknown

"Shifting My Focus"
Chapter 9:

Although things at work were changing for me, I decided to focus my attention on something else—my love life. I just couldn't seem to attract the perfect guy. My god mom always told me that I shouldn't be looking for my husband but waiting for him to find me, but for some reason, I had a hard time listening. One day we had a talk and she told me to go home and write down the things that I was expecting from my husband on a piece of paper. This assignment sounded so fun, and I couldn't wait to do it.

[My List:]

1. He can't have no kids.
2. He got to have good credit.
3. He got to be fine and tall.
4. He got to drive a nice car.
5. He got to have some money.
6. He cannot be a cheater.
7. He cannot be a street guy.
8. He got to go to New Life Church.
9. He got to be smart.

and the list went on.

"I can't wait to show Ms. Cassandra this list hunty because I crossed every t and dotted every I," I said to myself while checking over it.

The next morning, I called Bryant to see if he was coming to pick me up.

[Ring, ring, ring] "Hello," he said.

"Bryant you still coming to pick me up today," I asked as soon as he answered the phone.

"Lashonda, you know I'm coming. Be ready by 8:15 and don't have me downstairs waiting," he responded.

"Boy, stop playing with me. You know I'm going to be ready; you just make sure you are here at 8:15," I responded cracking up.

"Lashonda, you just like getting on my nerves, don't you? Now get off my phone."

"Bye," I said cracking up because I did love getting on his nerves.

-Fifteen minutes later-

[These the days of our lives, I'm living like I want to, stunting like I want to, winnings what I'm gone do] [song by Lil Durk] was on full blast as it came up the block. *"Bryant's downstairs"* I said to myself, rushing out the front door. Once I made it downstairs, I opened his passenger side door and yelled, "Boy, why you got this music bumping this loud early in the morning, waking up the whole neighborhood."

"Girl, this my car. Now hurry up and get in and put your seatbelt on so we can go," he yelled back because his music was that loud.

I started cracking up and said, "Okay."

While we were driving, I started paying more attention to the song that was playing and I asked him, "who is this BB, this song raw?"

"Why, you don't know him?" he responded.

"Bryant, I don't think I know any of the rappers that you listen to. Anyways, are we getting tamales this morning because I'm hungry?" I asked as we were getting closer to work.

"Yes Lashonda," he responded laughing.

We made it to SCI and on our way into the building, we started arguing about how to cross the street.

"Why are y'all always arguing?" Ms. Cassandra asked as she was walking towards the door to open it. "Y'all keep on and I'm going to put y'all in different cubicles," she said.

We walked through the door laughing, making our way to our desks.

"I'm about to go run and grab the tamales," Bryant said.

"Oh, BB, grab me some chips out of the vending machine too," I said as I took my coat off.

"Lashonda, I don't know who you think I am," he said laughing before he walked out the door. I started laughing to as I grabbed my list out of my purse to show Ms. Cassandra. I was looking forward to hearing her tell me how great I did.

"Here's my list Ms. Cassandra," I said as I handed it to her.

"Lashonda, what is this foolishness?" she asked as she started reading it.

I started cracking up and responded, "The list you told me to go home and make."

"Girl, you are tripping. You are asking God to basically send you a perfect man. You need to go home and redo this list and be more realistic," she said as she handed me my list back. I started cracking up again, walking back to my desk because I was not expecting the response that she gave me.

"Here you go Lashonda. They didn't have the chips you like in the vending machine," Bryant said as he handed me the tamales that he bought for me.

"Okay, thanks," I responded smiling.

"I'll be in the resource room if you need me," he said as he left again.

"Okay."

Bryant was always so nice to me, no matter how crazy I acted. He had the patience to deal with my foolishness. I smiled, counting down the hours until work ended because I wanted to go home and finish working on my list.

The next day, I presented my God mom with the revised version of my list and she still disapproved of what I wrote. "Ms. Cassandra, I don't get it. What am I doing wrong?" I asked her as we were walking into the town hall to sit down and have a talk.

"Well, first, you are not supposed to be searching for a man, he is supposed to be looking for you. The bible says, "he that finds himself a wife finds himself a good thing, not she."

"Okay," I said looking disappointed because I had to give up searching for my man. "I see I got a lot to learn," I told her.

She smiled at me and said, "Don't be disappointed, your husband will find you."

"What y'all in here talking about Cassie?" Bryant asked as he walked into the room, interrupting us. We looked at him and started laughing.

"None of your business," Ms. Cassandra said as she got up to leave and return to her desk. Bryant and I looked at each other and started laughing again, and we walked back to our desks to finish up our work before the day had ended.

"Sometimes, what you truly need is right in front of you, but you've got to be willing to open your eyes and see things in a different and better light."

-Sibyl

"In Denial"

Chapter 10:

Everyone always thought that Bryant and I were a couple because we were always together and always arguing about something. We were really best friends, but no one we knew was trying to hear that. Bryant had a specific kind of girl that he liked, and I knew for a fact that that woman wasn't me because I was from the projects and real life crazy.

"Oh, my gooooshh, hey cousin. What are you doing up here?" I screamed as I walked into the resource center to see my cousin Byron on the computers. I had not seen him in a long time.

"Heeeyyyyy cousin," he responded super excited. We greeted each other with hugs. "I came to use the computer to look for a job," he said. "Aw ok, let me log you in," I told him (y'all, my cousin is one of the greatest persons in the world and he is going to always be his true authentic self).

"Why you down here making all that noise Cassie Jr.?" Bryant said as he walked into the resource room.

"Stop playing with me," I said cracking up.

"Be-Be, this my little cousin."

"Who, Wesley Snipes?" he said referring to my cousin Byron and we all started laughing.

"I'm not no d*** Wesley Snipes," my cousin responded. "I know him already," Bryant added. They clapped hands and greeted each other. Bryant looked at me, smiled, and then walked back to his desk to sit down. "Girlllllll, he likes you," my cousin said looking at me smiling.

"No he don't cousin. That's my god brother," I responded.

"Girl, did you see how he just looked at you?" my cousin added.

"No, and that's just my best friend," I responded.

"Yeah okay," my cousin said.

"I'm about to run back to my desk real quick. I'll be right back," I told him.

"Okay," he said.

As I walked down the hall, I started smiling super hard thinking about me and my cousin's conversation.

"What are you smiling so hard for Lashonda?" Mr. Green asked as he walked pass me in the hallway.

"Oh, nothing. Hey Mr. Green," I responded still smiling. Once I was back at my desk, I grabbed the information that I needed and walked back down to the resource room to help my cousin. We stayed on that computer searching for jobs until it was time for us to go home.

As time went by during the next few months, Bryant and I grew closer. If I came to work, he came. If I didn't come, he didn't come and vice versa. If I wanted him to take me somewhere, he would take me. If I needed my trash taken out, he would do it. If he was about to take a long ride somewhere, I went with him. We were like two peas in a pot. He knew about every guy that I dated, and I knew about every girl he dated. I guess everyone was right. Bryant and I were a couple. I just didn't see it yet.

"How will you know if it's the right decision if you never make it?"

-Unknown

"A Decision to Make"

Chapter 11:

Because of the unrealistic list I created of all the things I expected from my husband, I found myself in and out of relationships because I compared every guy to that list. *"Either I am too picky, or these dudes just ain't acting right,"* I thought to myself as I was going through my phone. I needed to talk with someone else who was going to be straight with me and give me the truth that I didn't want to hear, so I decided to call my best friend Laquita. I knew for a fact that she wouldn't beat around the bush.

I tried calling her, but it went to voicemail. Once I heard that, I hung up and texted her:

"Hey Quita, call me when you get a chance. I need to ask you something."

A few hours later, my phone rang, and it was just the call I had been waiting for. "Hello,"

"Hey Shonda, what's up?" she asked after I answered the phone.

"Girl, I want to ask you something and I need you to be honest with me."

"Okay," she responded. "Do you think I'm too picky when it comes to men?"

"Yes, hell yeah," she responded in a serious tone.

I started cracking up as I realized in that moment that I was the issue.

"Now, why you say that?" I asked.

"Girl, you got everything you been looking for sitting right in front of you and you act like you can't see that."

"Who are you talking about Quita?" I asked.

"I'm talking about Bryant. Why won't you give him a chance?" she asked.

"Girl, you know Bryant is my godbrother," I said.

"Shonda, that boy likes you and you act like you can't see that," she responded as silence came over our conversation.

"You asked me to tell you the truth and I did."

"Okay, bye. I will call you later," I said. I got upset after hearing what she said because that wasn't the answer I was looking for. I couldn't stand being wrong. I honestly just wanted her to tell me that these guys were tripping, but it didn't go my way, so I ended the conversation.

"Okay, Quita and the rest of the world, y'all just might be right," I whispered as I laid on my bed, staring up at the ceiling.

Some weeks had passed, and I couldn't stop thinking about the conversation my best friend and I had. Questions and statements started flooding my mind. *"Is he what I had been praying for? Will we work as a couple? Nope, I think we are good as friends. I am not about to look like a clown listening to what everybody is saying. You know what, I'll just ask him for myself, how about that."* I decided to go over to Bryant's house one day after work and ask him the question that I wanted to ask. I was scared, but I mustered up the confidence to do it anyways.

Bryant had put on a movie for us to watch and I got super nervous. The little voices in my head just kept saying *do it, do it, ask him.*

"Bryant," I said super softly.

"Yeah?" he responded.

"Can I ask you something?"

"Yeah."

"Do you like me?" I asked quickly as we were staring at the T.V.

He turned his head, looked at me and said, "Lashonda, you know I like you."

I started cracking up because I was super shocked. I was not expecting him to say yes. I just knew that I wasn't his type because he liked girls that went to college and look like Rihanna. I smiled really hard and said "Boy, now how was I supposed to know that?"

He looked at me and said, "Why you think I was driving you around, and picking you up and putting up with your crazy self?"

I started cracking up even more and said, "Boy, I thought you was being nice to me."

"Yeah ok," he responded as we started laughing again.

"I don't want us to jack up our friendship because we didn't work out," I responded.

"Ok Lashonda. That's totally your decision to make. You asked me a question and I gave you an answer," he said as we resumed watching the movie.

"And oh, by the way, I ain't got no good credit, just so you know, its jacked up," he added and we both started cracking up. Once the movie ended, I decided to go home because I had a lot to think about, but most importantly, I had a decision to make.

F-E-A-R has two definitions:

1.) Forget Everything And Run

OR

2.) Face Everything And Rise

The choice is yours!

-Zig Ziglar

"A Decision"
Chapter 12:

"Okay Bryant, I made a decision about what I asked you and this is what I came up with. Since we have been friends for a long time and we know each other very well, we can just go ahead and get married," I said as I was pacing the floor back and forth in his room.

"HAHAHAAAAAAAAA, Lashonda, who do you think I am?" he responded cracking up.

"So you saying you don't want to marry me?" I asked staring at him with my serious face and my hands on my hip.

"That is not what I said crazy girl. I'm saying that we not about to get married and we haven't dated yet. We don't know each other romantically. Our friendship is only the foundation of our relationship. Whether we work or not, at least we will always be friends," he said.

"Okay, well, that does make more sense," I responded as I sat down on the bed next to him. "Well, if you do ever decide to propose, I want you to send me on a scavenger hunt and then we end up on a horse and carriage ride and you can propose in private. That way, if we don't work out, we cannot work out privately."

"Okay Lashonda," he responded laughing because he knew I was always going overboard.

From what you know about me and Bryant so far, you can probably see that our romantic relationship, didn't start off so romantically. It actually went a little like this.

"You get on my nerves," he would say.

"And you get on my nerves too," I would respond. "Look, I don't have to sit here and deal with your sh**, I can take my a** home (forgive my language y'all, my mouth can get real potty when I'm angry). Then I would storm out of the house all dramatically, slamming the door behind me, driving home listening to music that verified my anger, only to get a text message from Bryant minutes later that would say:

"Can you bring me something to eat?"

I wouldn't respond on purpose for ten minutes, then I would respond and say:

"Yes, what do you want to eat?"

I would go get the food, take it to him and then we would apologize to each other. A week later, we would be right back at it again. One day, we sat down to figure out why we argued so much and what could be done about it. We both realized that we went to work together, we took our lunch breaks together, we hung out with our friends together, we went to church together and we went home together. It was too much *togetherness* going on and we needed to figure out how to fix that. Thankfully, our grant from work was coming to an end soon and we had to find new jobs whether we wanted to or not. We vowed never to work together again, and we didn't. Our romantic relationship started to get a little better from then on.

Eventually, we moved in together after a few years. I did not let up about us getting married because we were shacking, and we knew better. One day, I told Bryant that we needed to get married, or I needed to move out and get my own place and we could figure things out from there. He took what I said seriously and sooner, rather than later, his response made it very clear where we stood.

"Say you'll never fall again. You won't subject yourself to such pain. If you give me half a chance I will, I'll never leave you standing out in the rain. But if you think that I could look you in your face and lie right through my teeth, then turn around and walk away. Cross my heart, girl I care for you, when I look into your eyes, I must say. I need you now, I'll show you how, I can be the man you need me to be."

Song by:
–Brian McKnight
"Only One for Me"

"Another Beginning"
Chapter 13:

On October 6, 2016 (my birthday, woo-woo), another beginning was about to take place. That morning, Bryant woke me up and asked me if I could drop him off at work. I immediately knew something was off. Bryant never asked me to take him anywhere because 1. He didn't like how I drove, and 2. I always took the longest routes. We made our way downstairs to get in the car and he said he forgot something in the house, so he ran back upstairs. I didn't think anything of it because it was normal to forget something. He came back downstairs; I dropped him off at work and then made my way back home.

Once I opened the door to our bedroom, I noticed a Victoria Secret bag and three roses laying on the bed along with a note. The note told me to go to Edible Arrangements and pick something up at 10 a.m. When I got there at the stated time, I noticed that there were another set of roses; three actually. There was also a box of chocolate covered strawberries (my favorite) waiting for me along with another note. Once I read the note, I immediately noticed that I was on a scavenger hunt. The same scavenger hunt I told Bryant to send me on if he ever wanted to propose. I got in the car, and I calmed my nerves. I didn't want to get my hopes up high because this might not be what I thought it was. I finished the scavenger hunt, went home and showered, then went to sleep. I couldn't wait until 5' o clock came so I could see Bryant and we can go and have dinner at one of my favorite restaurants.

Around 5:30 pm, Bryant finally made it home and I was so happy to see him. We started getting ready so we could make our way to our dinner reservations at the Grand Luxe Café downtown. Once we got in the car, I heard his mom say, "record it lil Bryant." I immediately said to myself *"girlllllllll, this is that."* We finally made it downtown and he parked the car. When I turned to look at him, he was sweating super hard.

I started cracking up and said, "Boy, is you ok?"

He wiped his forehead and said, "Yes crazy girl, I just need to ask you something."

"Okay, well ask me then," I said, staring at him smiling. He then went on to explain the reason why he left three roses at each spot he sent me to. I was amazed listening to what he was saying because I couldn't believe that he actually went through all this trouble to propose to me exactly how I asked him to. We couldn't do the horse and carriage ride because it was raining super hard. He then took a box out of his pocket and asked if I would marry him. I smiled super hard and screamed **"YESSSS!!!"** We got out of the car and made our way into the restaurant. I didn't even order or eat the food because I was too busy on Facebook posting about our engagement. Bryant had to keep apologizing to the waitress for me because I wasn't responding to anything she was asking. I was too busy responding to everyone else on Facebook. We decided that it would be best to just take our food to go.

Once we made it home, we told his mom, and his sisters, and my mom and my sisters about how everything had happened, and they all were super excited. They started making plans before we even came up with a date (l.o.l). Just feeling the love, and excitement from them made me joyful all over again.

We set the date for August 5, 2017 (my mother-in-law's birthday woo-woo) and the day had come for us to get married. I was more than excited. The whole process was an amazing experience. We had so much help from our families, friends, and co-workers. We got married in the same place where Angela Martin hosted her Onederful Prayer meetings. It was perfect. I wanted that spot because I knew the presence of God would be there and the way that Angela Martin prayed, bay-be, was everything. My husband made sure that everything I wanted, I got it, and he stopped at nothing to make sure that it came to past. Once the wedding was over, you already know what we went home to do. One year later, we had our handsome baby boy, and the rest is history. We are still together, looking forward to facing our futures together. I can see now that Jesus does work in mysterious ways; you just have to be open to them.

"Holy spirit activate. Holy spirit activate. Holy spirit activate, activate, activate."

-Chynna Phillip
"From the Steve Harvey Family Feud Show"

Now, I know that while you were reading this book, you may have thought that I wrote it about me and my husband, or maybe even about all those amazing people that helped me along the way, but I didn't. I wrote this book about Jesus and how he changed my life. You see, in some strange, amazing way, I believe that sitting on my aunt's porch, sulking in my feelings, was me being in the right place at the right time. I believe that God saw it as an opportunity to sweep into my life and take over. He drove up on me and encouraged me to keep moving forward. He pulled me into my destiny and when I was hesitant, he gave me a little shove to stop being afraid and face what was before me. He took care of me. He fed me. He made sure he put a roof over my head, whether it was mine or not. He led me back to him. He tested me. He checked up on me regularly. He kept it real with me. He even waited to reveal my husband unto me until I was mature enough to receive him. He forgave me even when I was doing things I knew I shouldn't have been doing. He is AMAZING, for all those reasons and more. He is my everything. I know that I would have never made it this far without Him.

So you see, the main character was never the main character, he was actually behind the scenes the whole time.

"The End"

Every tear your children cry

Every cloud in stormy sky

Everyone beat up by life

You make beautiful

Every valley I walk through

Every battle I may lose

Days when I gave up on you

You make beautiful

See all things together

Are working forever

A beautiful plan for me

So, make me beautiful

Make over my soul

Till the whole world know

You make everything beautiful

Song by:
-The Walls Group ft. Kirk Franklin
"Beautiful"

Thank you so much for reading my book. I hope you enjoyed it. You can visit my website @ **www.theleefam.net** to learn a little more about me.

"Love. Peace. Hair-Grease."

Made in the USA
Columbia, SC
12 December 2022